FOSFENI

ESSENTIAL POETS SERIES 177

This book was made possible through the support of the Istituto Italiano di Cultura/Italian Government Cultural Institute (IIC) of Los Angeles, Francesca Valente, Director; IIC San Francisco, Amelia Carpenito, Director; IIC Chicago, Annunziata Cervone, Director; IIC New York, Riccardo Viale, Director; IIC Washington, Rita Venturelli, Director; IIC Toronto, Martin Stiglio Director.

ANDREA ZANZOTTO

FOSFENI

TRANSLATED FROM THE ITALIAN
BY PASQUALE VERDICCHIO

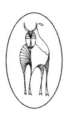

GUERNICA

TORONTO – BUFFALO – LANCASTER (U.K.)

2010

Antonio D'Alfonso, editor

Guernica Editions Inc.

P.O. Box 117, Station P, Toronto (ON), Canada M5S 2S6

2250 Military Road, Tonawanda, N.Y. 14150-6000 U.S.A.

Distributors:

University of Toronto Press Distribution,

5201 Dufferin Street, Toronto (ON), Canada M3H 5T8

Gazelle Book Services, White Cross Mills, High Town, Lancaster LA1 4XS U.K.

First edition.

Printed in Canada.

Legal Deposit – Second Quarter

Library of Congress Catalog Card Number: 2010926066

Library and Archives Canada Cataloguing in Publication

Zanzotto, Andrea, 1921-

Fosfeni / written by Andrea Zanzotto ; translated by Pasquale Verdicchio.

(Essential poets series 177)

Poems.

Translation of Italian book with same title.

Includes bibliographical references.

ISBN 978-1-55071-329-9

I. Verdicchio, Pasquale, 1954- II. Title.

III. Series: Essential poets series ; 177.

PQ4851.A74F6813 2010   851'.914   C2010-902340-4

THE PHOSPHORESCENCE OF
INIMITABLE SIGNS

Pasquale Verdicchio

This translation of *Fosfeni* has been in the making for many years, in the sense that I felt an immediate affinity to the writing and an urge to translate it when I first purchased it in Florence in 1984. But these things have their own time and so, aside from the publication of a few pieces (*Sulfur* 29, Fall 1991), it has taken over two decades for the project to finally come to fruition. It will not take readers long to recognize the difficulties that a work such as this presents. Translating these compositions, much like any translocation of a work from one language into another, means first of all to recognize the impossibility of a fully accurate transference into English. Zanzotto, himself a translator, has commented that: "Translation, the 'transference' of poetry in a total sense, is impossible; it is of course possible that one might achieve transplants, grafts, or some wonderful imitations, especially for a certain type of poetry that is based on and presents a fundamentally logical and flowing sense, relatable to some sort of transportability" (Zanzotto 1995, 27).

Among all the poetry that I have translated, *Fosfeni* stands out as being most representative of what might be considered a graft; neither less "accurate" than the original nor than other translations. Translating poetry is after all reading poetry and, as such, it implies a similar sense of interpretation, reconstitution and assimilation into one's own system of understanding. Translation offers the opportunity of losing one's self in the

5

enjoyment of the polyvalent intricacies of the poetic text; *Fosfeni*, by its very difficulty and apparent incongruencies, makes possible an extended and valuable interaction with language. Zanzotto's understanding of poetry, as something that should always leave "the conversation open, especially toward others and the 'other'" (29) is also an attitude that in effect makes possible translation. Never having been "too attached to the notion of a definitive poetic text" (29), Zanzotto offers readers a poetic practice that speaks to an engagement of language that falls outside the declarative and objective into the realm of experience and dialogue.

Working in a completely different linguistic and cultural context, the translator is required to make choices that often appear to negate the myriad meanings at work within the original. On the other hand, the inventiveness that translation requires in teasing out meaning and extra-linguistic correspondences, the obvious cultural differences and connotations, makes of the translator a co-author in the creation of something new. Works of the difficulty of *Fosfeni* give translators not only such a privilege, but also provide a deep lesson in language, communication and composition.

In hindsight, some of the difficulties presented by this work, the puzzling neologisms and linguistic playfulness, became a little clearer when I visited Zanzotto at his home in Pieve di Soligo. The peculiarities of his work were unveiled not as a result of any explanation that he might have offered, nor by clarification for which I might have asked. In fact, we spoke little of the book itself. What opened up the writing was Zanzotto's manner of speaking and the rhythms of his person as we strolled through his town. That is what provided flashes of insight (fosfeni?) into his poetic engagement with the landscape.

Fosfeni is the second book in what Zanzotto has referred to as a "highly improbable trilogy" (Zanzotto's *Notes* to this book). Published between *Galateo in bosco* (1978) and *Idioma* (1986), the poems of *Fosfeni* were written "mostly at the same time as those in *Galateo*, between 1975 and 1978. Others were added in subsequent years, until 1981" (*Notes*) and also represent a sort of compositional middle-point in the poet's six decades of poetic activity. The braided compositions, as it were, arising at the same moment as others that became parts of different collections, allow us a glance into Zanzotto's writing habits. During the course of an interview with Beverly Allen, the poet explains that he never plans anything: "I write when it happens. It comes as it comes, and I let it rot in my drawer, as it were… The first book to come out, which I have finished and which violently structured itself this way, is precisely this *Galateo in bosco*, which then continues in another book the title of which I don't yet see clearly, and a third book whose title I already do see: *Mistieroi*" (Allen 262-263). The middle book, the title of which Zanzotto has yet to "see clearly" will be *Fosfeni,* a title that refers to the "vortexes of signs and luminous points one sees holding one's eyes closed tight" (*Notes*)

Zanzotto explains that in his early books he sought to look beyond human presence in the landscape out of a form of distaste brought about by historical events such as World War II. While the landscape tends to take center-stage, as the poet attempts to imagine it free of man's actions upon it, he casts his gaze beyond the visible surfaces in order to begin to understand their appearance and our place within/among them. Beginning as a psychological reflex-re-action to the devastation of war, Zanzotto's first book *Dietro il paesaggio* (1951) introduces this singular poet as an enigma onto an Italian cultural scene that was strongly under the influence of Neorealism. And yet, if we consider the effect of

7

twenty years of Fascist rule and influence on all aspects of culture, in the manipulation of language toward normative and solidified meanings, Zanzotto's poetics becomes indicative of a continued resistance. This too becomes another suggestion of new possibilities and directions in a post World War II Italy struggling to regain its footing.

From the point of view of what we might consider to be an "environmental" reading of this poetry, regarding the social, cultural and political landscapes as they had been altered by Fascism, the correspondences cannot but slide away from semantic certainties. Rather than singularly independent entities/meanings this poetry flows toward the interaction of innumerable, indescribable and impermanent forces that are in/the landscape, the *intergamie*/interranges ("Silica, Carbon, Scaffolders"), or the connections that range through and across the landscape and everything in it:

> Parables avalanche to avalanche, in episodes,
> clouds of filaments, limpid predicates
> produce and reconnect at will
> in the cleared orb by never-more
> cleansed in silica
> in carbons and other rarities
> And the tenuous tavern bill
> that some, and the I that everyone says of themselves,
> wanted to open up there on the knob

> *Silica, Carbon, Scaffolders*

If it is at all possible to generalize about Zanzotto's poetics, it could be said to be a poetry centered around the relationships of the various linguistic possibilities open to a human biological/existential presence. This is in turn directly but loosely tied to the historical evolutions of poetic languages and forms. His reconsiderations of these traditions in *Elegia e altri versi* (1954), *IX Ecloghe* (1962) and *Galateo* (1978), where Dante, Petrarca and others loom large, seek to extend and test their limits: "In fact, I've had two compasses: first the Petrarchan compass and then the Dantesque, a 'first' and a 'then' that also correspond to an evolution of my own language" (Allen 253).

Zanzotto's undoing of institutionalized forms of communication in *La Beltà* (1968) have been said to bring him into line with the poetic innovations of the *I Novissimi*.[1] The actions of this innovative group of writers on form and language were often regarded as having been mostly terroristic and destructive in nature. While this assessment is most likely the result of the political and cultural context in which the writers worked, and was to a certain extent true, today it has mostly been re-contextualized and corrected. Their target was Italian as a standardized (and therefore fictional) language that was not thought to properly reflect how language in Italy had been forming under the influence of industrialization and social changes. An example of this are the writings of Nanni Balestrini, which illustrate the example of what might constitute a developing linguistic reality as a mix of Italian, the technological language prevalent in industry, a Marxist vocabulary of resistance and political consciousness that had acquired currency among workers, and the variety of dialects that brought into play those of southern workers migrated north with those of the local workers. Or Antonio Porta's *Metropolis* (1971), with its effacement of common-place beliefs and assumptions. While Zanzotto did indeed share with *I Novissimi* an adamant dislike for the neocapitalist and consumeristic culture that was shaping post-war Italy in its "economic boom" period, Zanzotto's work has distinguished itself in a number of ways.

While also intending to disrupt accepted linguistic hegemonic conventions, his language emerges and moves through linguistic alternatives such as *petèl* (baby-talk), the dialect of the Veneto region and more specifically the dialect of the town and region in which he lives. Foremost among his concerns is the need to reassess the function of the writing subject, the first person "I." Zanzotto's interest in the "I" is engaged in rescuing it from its emphatic function as a dominant pronoun and establishing it in the landscape as a noun, as opposed to *I Novissimi*'s attempts undermining its authoring/authoritative stance through erasure.

Fosfeni (1983), as an exploration of the movement from *topos* to *logos*, their blending of positions and interplay, is one of Zanzotto's most complex collections. The shift from *topoi* of accepted norms toward a *logoi* that vibrate with the flash of *fosfeni* (phosphorescences) is "the only actual reality [to be found in] the linguistic signifier, in its continuous reference to new possible formulations of a meaning that slides away from the possibility of being fully confused with the signifier"(Fabbri 91). The shifting signifier, not attached to any particular signified, or to its own sense of direct signification, is representative of the *logos* as a diminishing centripetal point. The collection's recurring trope (images of *ice*, *gel*, *crystals*, *creams* and *gelatins*) supports the sense of fluidity that Zanzotto evinces from language:

Tiger november meanwhile and always it prowls
throws everything at the feet the astral happy disaster
uses as arms the moonscythe and sunscythe
it causes the leap of colors the disaccord or chorus –
makes pleural drainage for skins and hyaline strata and gel
pours crystals misplaces a finger of wine
on the table for two

From *Knick-knacks and Gel*

Ice, creams and *gels* are all substances that change state and form to repeat themselves and conform to ambient conditions, by which they communicate the qualities of their environment. Just as *ice* communicates water and all its other states, so words communicate a context and a sense of their relation not only to a language or a grammar as conventions but as lived experience.

The bi-directional flow diagram auto ⇔ bio ⇔ graphy, offered by Zanzotto in a piece written just before the release of *Fosfeni*, expresses the movement of language in the poetic process, where the biological body is the point of intersection.[2] "Last Suppers," which opens the collection, presents a finality that, in its repetition of the Platonic symposium or the Biblical banquet *ad infinitum,* nevertheless offers an open ended poetic dialogue and the provisions to fuel that exercise. Its overall effect is to enact a continuous renewal of discursive tendencies that reverberate throughout the cultural landscape.

Zanzotto refers to this poetic process of ingestion, reconstitution and repetition as a "revomiting," something that in a North American context might remind us of Charles Olson's remark that "diet precedes language." After a close association with the body, the ingestion of language conventions returns poetry as a varied assortment of graphemes, phrases, letters, and verses. This gelatinous by-product, the consolidation of disparate elements into terms of expression, is the substance that gels in the pages of *Fosfeni*. The gel, gelatin, and ice consolidate *topos* and *logos* as they leave the body, to rejoin and alter the landscape as a coating that covers the ground with an accumulation of transformational poetics upon which we tread as readers.

11

Notes

1. The avant-garde group *I Novissimi* consisted of writers who initi-
ated a poetics of renewal in contrast to Italian canonical literary
tradition. Their experiments and proposals sought to identify and
reproduce a language representative of the cultural mixing and
hybridity that was beginning to take shape in "economic boom"
Italy. The migration of millions of southerners to northern indus-
trial cities led to a meeting of southern dialects with northern
dialects, standardized Italian, industrial technical jargon and the
vocabulary of Marxist revolutionary ideology that these new
workers were beginning to acquire as they explored their rela-
tionship to the neo-capitalist industrial situation in which they
had been thrown. *I Novissimi* published an anthology by that
same name in 1961 which included the work of Antonio Porta,
Edoardo Sanguineti, Alfredo Giuliani, Elio Pagliarani and
Nanni Balestrini. This grouping worked toward the eventual
founding of the more inclusive and multi-faceted *Gruppo '63* in
1963 among whom were included artists, film makers and
philosophers.

2. Zanzotto's contribution to the volume *The Favorite Malice*, pro-
ceedings from a symposium held at NYU in 1979. Pages 131-157.

BIBLIOGRAPHY

Allen, Beverly. (1984). "Interview with Andrea Zanzotto (Pieve di Soligo: July 25, 1978). *Stanford Italian Review*, IV, 2. Fall 1984. Anma Libri. (253-265).

Fabbri, Pierluigi. (2000). *Andrea Zanzotto: Itinerario critico per una poesia possible*. Collezione Oxenford – 108. Firenze: Firenze Atheneum.

Harrison, Thomas J. Editor and translator. *The Favorite Malice*. New York: Out of London Press, 1983.

Zanzotto, Andrea. (1984). *Fosfeni*. Lo specchio. I poeti del nostro tempo. Milano: Mondadori.

———. (1993). *Andrea Zanzotto: Poesie (1938-1986)*. A cura di Stefano Agosti. Oscar poesia. Milano: Oscar Mondadori.

——— . (1995). *Europa, melograno di lingue*. Società Dante Alighieri, Comitato Veneziano. Università degli Studi di Venezia.

LIKE LAST SUPPERS

Nocturnal March thirst,
dry countryside   razed cold
    like a beard
    shaven every urge of levitation
and everything leavened and comprehended
                 in the cold,
          partner in the cold
dust is gel,   so dry from thirst, in the headlights,
in the shavings we find   don't bark
the road the turnoff – sneeze –
bothered gibbous crescent, empty loads
loaded streets and then field grasses emptied palate
    and much too responsible for invention   don't bark
not night, but a start in the night,
roads which the least little thing hastened to die
to be more chaste more deserving for an instant
    to be a headlight
    or a glare of nothing-glass   don't bark

Like going through the back door
in the sweet composition of a last supper
more painting – fits and starts outside – than
one might breathlessly dream, envy –
like the necessity of sublimation
no rays no relief no pretense
in any case everything excellently content in its non-being
actually a sort of N.N.N. in gel in alcohol gel
Supper in the cold defended only by itself
supper where it is always useful to stick one's foot

where meats viands victuals and milk and cappuccino
where golden drug of supper settles
    effuses into an emersion of itself faces con-figurations
    caters to no-one and itself, precarious composition,
    accessible initiation   miniorgasm in atchoo
warmish with initiation in in zzz of sleep razor
warm hole   (insinuations) (indicators)
                sacred coagulation (gossip)
of initiation, of paupery, resignation to scarcity
    puppets
most beautiful in the least
cheap turgidity, stare caught in the laces
of victuals and trays of table fruit, not even dining hall
    There are no dining halls here   razor
but only blood-foods and irritable ice creams
and tavern-girl who skirts away
        and Circeic circuits, highly anxious toys
If I were to theorize a face if I were
    to give up at dissymmetry (if I)
of a convolvulus of face in its own blondness, dry rain,
of nestling beauty-ty-go-gel   razor
golden threads inside a lamp, beneath a violent memory:
    scarce words and scarce lines, all friendly-like,
    traveling, head resting,
    sleep, rest settled on everything,
    melding into everything in sleep,
    startled along divinely ruined streets

    Hadn't seen much around for a while
    of the delicate, the after-face,
    a while since I last unwrapped a face from the face,
    a while since I last subtracted, since I cleaned up

a while since I was last startled in the car
balance of groves and countryside, false pool table
clinking betrayal and real ahi of locks for last suppers
"Which conditioner do you like for your hair?"
hairdresser-do last
supper at the edge of fields, tavern
"Which nail polish?"
girl, tavern (beneath the dust)
(beskance) (begold) (behair and who knows what)
"Which detergent absorbent for underthings, those
outside
under the stars   or those?"
and so many sweet formalities

ΘΕΩΙΑ ΚΡΥΟΣ

* * *

Impossible loves like
hills are actually impossible
It is not possible that so much love
in them could so openly be
given
and at the same time dissimulated,
    actually made inaccessible

    Series without remains of inaccessibility
    that is nevertheless captivating
    ingrading carpet on the
    largest breccia insanity disuse
    Hills rich with a thousand deadly dangers
        for   quietly
        for   precipitous aid
                                    among skytudes
        for   insufficient attention to itself –
        from fate to fate
        "will hinder"   "will defile itself"

SILICA, CARBON, SCAFFOLDERS

Oh if for all a bond
a vague distant eros
like a handshake
expired in a gray dawn...
                    (Silica, carbon)

From one tavern to the next, on peaks
not even sharp, but equally
sublime, in pale oh
no longer obscene no longer purification,
pale birth, on the wake of examples
    of flint-lock stones, kernels
    of pomegranate, tiny insects, calm
    and beautiful to settle
    the most attenuated non-divisions and interranges
    in almost abyssal sleep of dawn consumed
    or a blow of bright endured flint –
    for us furtive in a time of
comfort, gray comfort and gray closures

Or in worn purple, like a dissipating fever,
seemed right to cultivate
logos in carbon   logos in silica
like marginless loss here to generate present
    to educate
    dream of day-to-day
    sympathies of sympathies
    nervine, rather sullen syntonies

***

Great creativities
    anomalize the horizons
fresh contacts like to brine-greens...
But from where all is hoarse of shadows and collapse
calls the désir pirhana, the caritas
always at the stake, concupiscence
    of the skies of skies – the worst –
    calls the great religion of love
    that would throw up the tepid gray or
    light blue where furtive hands
    touch in the if-not-today-tomorrow.

He who wandering about ridges
wanted everything only as gentle
minimal offer of credit
"nothing is owed for this beautiful announcement"
who? From derma to derma
from down to down, oh
always held back at that point and truly
    infinite non-love
    an oblation of the power of reality
    sealed pact of lips and crust and humus
    seen everywhere
    even upon most distant peaks
    in the most intense aggressions of grass at the extreme
    in the most unusual
    hints of everything-everyone
    from his – as if inaccessible – sexual apparati.

Who was deceived by that chaste tonguing

who by those tenuous murmurs? Who
believed one day in the vanishing diaspora
of spring and promise, spring
because bride-crowd
                    dear to the gray?
Who practiced interranges along every synapse
                    every element every mathesis?
Who convened benignly into comet
ravines of leaves, sorcery of snows, human gazes?
Who opened the lapsed erotic cineteque to the public?
Who, with the mere teasing of a feather, saved
    the nostrils ear-lobes nipples the
    hypophysis, who saved?
But with these hilltop strides I will go
    to the first relationship with endless ice
    with untrustworthy divining vertigo
    preaching every non-religion
    every conversion or conversation,
    not preaching, not preaching, falling I will go.

***

So many, in framing circles, thoughts,
came from great
westerly, how many, among these homes-speakables,
    phases of love understood
    only improbably,
    cotamed impulses
    subtended resections! So much parabola of turgidity
    and parable of the shattered jug
    by the well
    and of fall-through essences
    in a shivering bitter blue
    at every valley, beyond every
    cohesiveness abstraction strength of silica! carbon!
        Oh calls quieted
                so sweetly: wait! Wait!
But the tavern door is bolted
        number one number two
        knocking   knocks with fists
                in vain
        to braid it into profiles, fables,
        memories of interranges
Parables avalanche to avalanche, in episodes,
clouds of filaments, limpid predicates
produce and reconnect at will
in the cleared orb by never-more
cleansed in silica
in carbons and other rarities
And the tenuous tavern bill
that some, and the I that everyone says of themselves,

wanted to open up there on the knob
to stimulate the nipple with a feather
and spread evangelical salts
beyond the precipice of elements
and grasp like good little thieves
hands, fingers in the gray,
or in the subtle accent of blueness
or in the much inhibited pleading
however-much hoarse
at the territory its
                    always marvelous silence.

Collapse and pomoerium

Tell me what I have lost
tell me what I have lost myself in
and why so much, everything
    I left at the foot of the wall –
    oh bundles caskets gatherings of brambles and then there
    twin lights, auriculations in the infinite pomoerium

I always stumble over it, something struggled over
defeated rebel in any case muto-dislocations
                  in flashes of the pomoerium
Tell me which and what way to collapse
Tell me which tongue I lost and left to collapse
Tell me in which tongue I lost I collapsed
    and why within this enclosure loved for its extreme
    loss
    I wandered without ever becoming lost
    nevertheless I was lost by some by some
Tell me so that every nerve of the greenest grass up
from the collapsed field of walls and pomoeria
    might perceive that which I do not
in the discredited, in the collapsed, in the simil-born
in which I earned and repeated myself
    Tell me why this estrangement always
    brings me face to face with love thought lost
    and on the back of forever I
    distance myself from the love thought lost –
    loves gathered up like threads of spit,
    invasion, place possessed taken
    completely by turning to my hiatus

Tell me: then it no longer matters: leaning on the pomoerium
unevenly, with unbalance or expulsion from the high state
of the heavens: force a thousand coins
suck a thousand preys offered illuminations
I started there something of mine
flowing in front of me
to qualify depth-ruin
worlds, glaring divine latrines –
adapted myself to you devoted
and humble demarcations of territory
laid down by what is more chemically animal –
    and you opened incalculables before me
leading me to collapsed skies their palpitating
                               deficits!

Tell me why in adoring this dry loss
or reducing more I cannot   or reducing
and that's all
or
paying no attention to remission, loan, substitute, oh,
like curled up curled up
or spread out spread out
from my own collapse I evolved
so that I could with my basest parts
of the dark's gleaming assume the true state
and finally raise orality and oration
be – in them – chemical sign   swollen pommel
never before identified
in the flight of evening of the
    released the freed the defenestrated
        beyond lips and nostrils
        on pomoerian instability
        of legend of agenda   and luminaries

(Loghion)

I uproot you like a weed
with great suffering, in your useless snaking
but so wise that not vegetable but with ommatidia
               rather with optic fibers
    you seem, or who knows what else

Or if you squat in the binding
perfectly little treatise of which I notice the spine
      emerge in the wandering course of the filth

Or sweet firefly, bubola or phosphoric borboleta,
   busily blinding me with cheap
     science-fiction pyrotechnics –
        in shadows no longer worth a dime –
not to speak of the acetylene torch airs you give yourself
     dragon that a child's breath could extinguish

Or again, basket of twigs   sparse –
place of arte povera   of bricolage
or litany of frightened millipedes
   that squirm hesitate but do not settle down, result of too
   many feet

You less expert that when the bird nests
and is too much an engineer
less efficient than when
   the hen gathers water and
     arranges sand in mounds

Use and exchange value
as much as there can be ground-level and shadow-level
as much as among the down of an ashen Lent
Uncertain tool asset of uncertain use
    incautiously connected here and there
    to a hand a foot that it avoids mistakes

    They cling like to forest incantations
now, now – stems break off – after after
    and cross in the wind
    at first light on the lanes

You poor among the poor, wounded among the wounded
crossroads of valences, instants, thesis   ephemeral –
    swallow tails, in hedges, slightly glanced

and memory lapses, breaks, leaks held back by a finger

MARTENS, PAINS, ΛΟΓΙΛ

Easter, you, mutable   (toward the undone, in the mute)
  always, maybe, the most mutable of all
    most marten of all holidays, most unsearchable
      in the net of junk bric-a-brac-holes and grasses
        you sheared netting, to the definitive, among
          moons   gravity   dispersed photos   atonements

Easter, useless to chase you
  useless the chase where
    you always falsify braid even and uneven
      paper and lantern under paper and lantern you hide
        they bragged
          disseminations of green chaff and ashes to
            succeed – and exit, moment, on the roundness
            of the Easter moon

You were not there, uninhabiting, never coinciding
  either with yourself or with other bite or
    sip of coincidences, in the most upright
      angle of
        negation wringing hands   spiniform burglaries

twirling of dirty turpentine in a swirl –
  quiet flight   or aggressive stamping of
    martens in sequins on patrol between
      rains, skating out of photo
        until night, until the comb of exhausted snows
          then sighted in full
            moon

Martens, pains, and the shot with silencer
   barely at feather-level, of chicken coops, of snows
     between deaf sets and silence: yes, I appear to be
       out of it, chh: every out chh: feud instigations chh
        moonanimous at night
          corners of honeycomb snow (last)
          or hermitages-of-me

Oh in vain among many start-overs
   or you up to your ear, to cautious eve... you believed me?
     or never fallen in the trap ever – from moon to moon...
     You meddler trip others toward nothingness
      we persecute you through flowering peaches and snows
       you de-flesh claws of rains from the hill
        frustrate and undo everything from everything
         and you take me and all the darkest pains with you

Pained pains, death dead, mine, my, without
  reference stability no longer
  mine – neither yours – nor theirs –
   figures, saintly, or mythical
    (meddler marten of a thousand diverging snouts)
     in the already teetering text, in the towns in pain
      in the betweengoings pains that no longer know
       that are no longer mine their own of nothing.

ΛE   ΛE

Variety of pink and yoni

1   Frosted place of wisterias
    where
    the hen pecks at petals and then makes honey
    of feathers and eggs
    no less than bees make forest,
    where where
    every aim becomes sustainable
    and every donative presentifies itself
            like crepuscular unlimitedness
            cocreative
    now the striker – cracrak – on your face
    struck rebounds, knocks you over   *now*
            from the counter, from the bust
            and then
            for which
            for which terrain breaks
            or even gentle slopes
                    you are convened, ruled,
            and you break up at random
            in search of knowing   *then*

2   Heart that gives off frost
    and street sweetness
     wobbling in a buggy
    between kicks and elbow blows
    beyond the greased poles –
    with fists relaxed

with head hanging
with unsoothed iris –
to no longer be at all any more
"a thousand possibilities in the evening"
neither god-ray nor resting muscle
nor mandibular protrusions
that tribulates as it warbles

Heart that gives off frost
body undone
in street sweetness
          out of season, reason

3   So exorcising the body
     that maybe connects you
     with the other beautiful one of the spring mat
         but ahi! Unprismed!
         Invaded by Antigens by Diabolicals by In vain!

4   There he is saddening, in a single moment,
     flitting up from the soft device bloodred
     from the plasma of pseudo-knowledge
     the photofinish
     That juice, that squashable, that pink...
     Frosts, frosts in narrows   Rose...
     A crystallography strips itself naked
     of everything, finally, painlessly,
     then yoni and that's all, drifts
     of never never ascertainable splendor

5 And you readjust yourself to your (a little
   exclamative)   visionality
   of chandelier of knick-knack
   of findus decalcomania
   You pull up over the scrim again
        the whole element
        In the ocular orbs
        resuck every wind stylus
        every disposition to blind
   Or you handle something that seems
        primed within the stabilizer –
        logic *then, where,*
        like pompeian cast plaster
        here in fact – but you must! you must!
        Among things! And all is beautiful! Even if
   frosts come to aid come to aid from everywhere
   antibodies come to aid
   to block such a story, in other words.

MORCHET THE TEACHER LIVES

Rubbing my, on a rainy day –
rubbing, or almost, from my eyes: but, but...!
 the teacher Morchet on the street
 in a very youthful skirt
 very eternal
 almost American with her bare legs at eighty
 almost participatory of a power
 almost a queen even if of a miserable
  rain-rotten day
  now of May
  yes, of May, for the pukeintessimal time
  "repeat, children, repeat"
"go to remedial class, Nice and All, to the teacher's"
Then, there is no doubt!
 She Wanders like the Hedges, She Distinguishes herself
 is slightly out of the hedge   branches illegally
  and   I resign myself to it etc. etc.
    rubbing my eyes branching out
     WE 2   porcupines both
       in a certain sense
We pretend not to follow or chase
yet we hoard and sulk
    but on two different sides of the street

Diverges from her own gold medal Torn (slightly)
appears to flutter and then Re-enters
more than in that my-poem of
more than ten years ago   Continues
in the gulp!   that it produces   and in the interregna too

and in the nebulous rubbing of rain-eyes
may be quoting Dante or rustling leaves
pushed aside by the robust arm
moved by the American skirt
    cloudy is the road asphalt
    meditations rise from it, Zen-gray incantations
    I would stop here make a tuft but no:
    make a chain, now, of buckets hand to hand,
    it is time for waters, for hydrogen, for devilfire

Oh Teacher, bygoshbygumbygod, bygosh,
    allmightysaintsofgod:
Walks through the deluge of rain
    godchildchristofgod!
She Walks – it is logical, didn't we know? –
    barely touched mediating wet streets,
        the earring rich hedges, the foreign pothole
        divined in a hundred thousand poems
            inextricably   and – full
            of fullness -   .   .   .   .   .   .

The statute has been communicated, hung to
every leaf-drop-larva
    larvae even apple-trees and where
    where the Reading Center was
    the washed washed smokexpansions
    spring in bucketfuls
    larvae even the reduced reducing to bones and nerves
and, let it be clear, :all of us and you are
    here less quotations
                    than proverbs
                    (proverbs of teacher-rains braided

thanks to rustling skirts)

This, Meeting, Street,
May, Morchet, Culture, Repeating Nature,
   straight and narrow like this, not at all insolent
   the final flight, eye-popping, blunt,
                     behind the teacher
                  who nevertheless has fooled every street
(to speak bluntly)   (a trace here or there)

looks askance   over her dentures –
   logical, no? The teacher will confirm
   our mise-en-abime that the label will require.

(Carillons)

And toward the end
of the uncoordinated banquet, sulphuric, chitterlings,
we noticed nothing was left – virtue of the carver! –
        if not a badly dissected apparatus
            to bid farewell to ourness
                ours because it had passed

At night: in the immense excited dark
    – after the revomiting of the unhappened banquet –
    in the dark where we wait
    where we are always awaited
    with silent enthusiasm
    with gelid enthusiasm and ignorance worthy of wonder
        but all for us, all for us (I feel it)

And she the ΠΑ was nothing more
    that life understood as a
    lo-
    very long and somnambulant goodbye to herself
    to to   that continuously
        in the carillon dissection
            reveals itself on the wall
                like an aficionado

9-6-75 (there where peaks are cruel)
I hear this date
as if naturally of place 75
        what? me to? do? have? to?

9-6

75   ?

Date beneath which to crawl

or maybe pedal by buries

(pass by, lottery, number of dead)

75-6-9

EUROSIA

Virgin, widow, Eurosia
        glorious one not of lightning but of hail
        pressed, spent firebolt that accumulates
        in alleyways is then recycled
                salt of the sunset,
                unimaginable start

So that the whole World might shine of actants
      and hailing photoreceptors
           real cats and diamonds
           preparations of astral valleys
           and astral comparisons

Pharmaceutical-Photons therapeutize
every vibration through hedges and gloom with
invisible and visibility deserving of eons
Optic fibres toward the most
hidden dreams and fruit and among the most beautiful
    theorems
skim understand each other

And the sister to the world, salt-on-salt
              grains-on-grains
              wrung here by my savage will,
and the sister of the world, saved,
with blessed Eurosia begins the vigil
so that everywhere pharmaceutical
from roots of optical fibers
           from hailstones

from tears
therapeutic only if one wants it.

This is how it happens, like this pedaling –
pedal on the edge on the lip on the corner
    while pebbles intervene and shadows
    fluttering from aspens and valued green for green
Pedal, foot by foot
    and leg by leg,
    ossifies, pedaling, takes tarsus and shins
Cascades of butterflies sponsor you,
proceed to the encounter in counter direction
pedal and push breathless worse than childbirth
between bright birthings of suns like butterflies
and between butterflies birthing gentle comments
Pedal and press like on grapes
and bend over the grapes
before you, mundane, conniving, fidelity
Recover recover and give
    in prize, go beyond anxieties and carnality:
    press bone-hard   sweetness from sourness from lucrative
    thefts
Pedal without trilling that no-one
the skipping flight on gravel among butterflies
        will hinder no-one

The squaring-off of the page has begun –
by kicks   well pedaled.

DISTRUST THROAT, BODY, MOVEMENTS, THEATRE

I

1 I'd like to leave, me
    I'd like to leave, you
        not aimless wandering nor living in line
        too much for certain-these-vocal-chords
        and in any case I stay out of it
    I'd like to suppress
    I'd like to rescind
    I'd like to intuit me in swarms in flocks in crowds
and place and carry out   Blue gold   Pluriblue

2 Blue doubt   blue certainty that does not pierce at all
    Ultracold, suggestions of cold
        l   l f leaf ea a
        And drip in warmth and color
        of multiblue-gold candle
        But dusts of wind-rose extinguish-like larynx
        Every exaltation prohibited equilibrated devolved
                in cold-storage and springs blue-gold
    In the dilemma of the tree TREESTRIPS
    In the voice (between us) that concerns bird TRAPS
      for   causal skies and water falls
                and flows following undone zippers

3   I'd like to desist to win back
    I'd like two hundred I'd like   a thousand, glowing,
    suddenly
    Store approach them and then store them
    and then instead find gloss-password
    between felt and felt and wood stingy wren

4   Oh shake yourself off   flay gold from the fitters
    don't you see that moon-paths spin toward every part
            Useless   behind... (gag, bit)

5   Intuition and desperation such close twins
                    so subtly inoculated
                    recoated in bacterial gold, of toothpick
            Who knew? Who said it?
            To know now – of poaching – abstracting from
                fronds of consensus, from gnawing the line

1   Ch. M., J.M.L. and others
Distrust the body make every action faint from hunger
Although those bodies, all too terrestrial, all too astral,
might crowd together oh, finally understood, like
TREES with asterisk (repeated above and below the line
    in isolation and in the plot
      by millions of eons X millions of mountain eons)...
        They (the trees) are cautious in announcing
    themselves and tritritri trii
    and much slower than how I heard them triii triii
                              oh irradicolarity iniity
All this – even – too will transcend me
even if, at times, I felt like sated by it   or clumsy triii
In qualifying myself   in the middle documents in hand
    I did not subdivide myself   up to the barter-door
        of self-service
I wanted even more and more maximums and minimums
    and good conduct
    and high-frequency offensive-defensive
    To install and camouflage myself forever, calculated
    forever,
shoved in the middle of the immense exterminability
    and participate in pouring and shaking downward
            libels of science and glory
            virginal vegetable cruelty
Never any dance but that of agony
No chords or vocal membranes
                    nor impulse of press-body-sebum
                    nor undoing of body in scales and dashes
Or at least trees in agony... Against...

In an autumn that drowns in its gold swim
he pulls the overloaded cart of sacks and wood shavings
carries on his shoulders
        a mendicant's sack with reflector
        among maniacally pure dusts
dusts and trees trees   Oh
oh miserable and blessed
you free of any desire to guide
        raise brandish the poker

Yaro-phano-gram no more no less
        left between broom bristles
Are not tree ideologies nor do they have
status as dynamic directions
for some hypothesis of musicality
        nor of reductions to intimacy
        for every and any dispersed finintimacy
        But the sack with the reflector rings and
I am here in my soup
  in my hot dish
        with blot ants manure flies
                before autumn: let's go in!
Oh only my inching tree trii
for the bleeding count
        yes
        yes, you grabbed her peduncle

by the caudal raddle
For the count of the cogito/sleep, rhizomes of sleep
　　　　　　　Nor is there time... and I have had so much,
　so much!
　　　　But who knows... yawn... there is time, nice weather
　　　　and strengths　　　and good　　　and mother of
truths
　　　　At the self-service gas station
　　　　where and trees trees arrive　　　　　still

FIRES

We have not just been blabbing away till now

　　　Drop　　　　　Drip face in the plate.

GOALS

Low shots ‖   ‖ skies lights ‖
                goal score aaah
and retracts sibyls needle snail
blind stumps ‖   ‖ sweats cold ‖

        silence that alters course ‖   that ‖

to empty belly skeleton straw
to the porosity of gold-want
to the compact of sky-lived
            low blows
that the context might develop
be repeated in every challenge
mark itself viscera/crimes
low shots   ssst!   and synthesis
or such dense wonder as not to explode
or usualness
            but turn to night distract incalculable
Divest of schema and scenes
Low shots   blood flow   ‖ that ‖
            look-bruise-of-larvae
    – Stiffens tight-bellied
    adheres fast to the sheet
    grassy dusty eroded by nights
        and days   divinant magical trade winds
The falling has slowed
the event   well filamented
            has leveled itself, below,
for a low shot

skillfully ‖ teeth ‖ collected

Low shots now stellar lessons
Stellarity of things
outstretched in nonsense in aged
            ambitions   purity → document

‖ and sweats cold-well ‖

Low shots in the veil
            in the veto

(At Ghène's)

Impossible to access the sweet ruin
of the tavern immobile at the corner
of the two roads turned toward the hoar frost
of autumnal old age and acquiescent gravels,
immobile like enchanted vignette

in the gnomes' journal

in the heroes' journal

in the journal of great sounds –
No temporality in the
walls that still
hold a trace of a comfortable, profound self,
and adapt and approach
open to a tender, intense reason.
visible panels and collapsed walls
beams and roof tiles of mutual support

so that the imperfect

shifts all together, but accentuated,

exalted beyond all habits

beyond all security –

light curtain or hell door

or door of limbo-vignette

Calm and certainty in your infinite undoing

in the beams that hold each other

up with difficulty in cinder blocks

already taken or torn by me one by one

in bricks that trust themselves to mortar

still, discolored, synthesis of coloration

of pardon, of restoration

Reconnoitering your black hollows
sometimes by those who pass by,
    but there is no mystery that lasts
    that does not purify in lime and mortar
    for slightly wandering eyes
    or thrown down with the creek
    or nested worse than any bird in there
    still – o dear ruin –
    welcomed by you along with the panoplies
    of inviting signs – always –
    BEER AND WINE a threat
    or subtle
    or demented proclamation.
Who would dare contradict?
Who not stop on this edge?
Who not taste, in passing, this yolk
of orders and space
contested in vain:
    is the data not all here??

Well disposed silences
undeburiable
but nevertheless dispersed in
nude sparkling
or in blind little fogs
ordered
Silences always innovated
and nevertheless in extended fidelity
within innumerable extractions of time
Subtracted silences
from every speculation, intent on itself
unaiding – nevertheless
well associated to love – crowd
Omnipresent in contingencies
and in continuous disparate provenance:
where suffering was just and without allusions
where the offer was undoubtedly οὐδεν απεϪπιζονσα

PERISCOPES

1

Accumulated years, like stones
    thrown haphazardly down there
oh so much blue in the blue
thickened by those throws
even if it is purulent with eternity –
    in that down there
And I who am here purulent in time
and stiffen my hands by dirtying and casting off years,
clapping, now, my hands
prepare the soil in liquid crystals
most vibrant, transcolored, astonishing
toward all the tints and limits:
a circumstance not to be missed, supreme.
Oh blue purulent of eternity
heap, then, of entities
emerged in the sun
through single appeals that have,
truly, year by year,
made incomprehensible, my hoped for comprehension

Sickened by verbal people, of first-persons
but not of accumulating accumulating down there
    color years and other false virtues
    definitely, with no way out,
    settled in its own in the mold

still I see distorted through an effervescence of suns
dripping
dregs of honey, sticky in its making
the most cruel imperversion of
                    mundane photon goods say yes

2

Valves, shutters, windscreens shift
now the most ogre chores among the ravines
        that I supported like children in the dews
        and then propped-up with my shoulders for many
    seasons
I see its amazement, its chameleontics
    useless within its uses
    of terror encounters couplings
    like of mineral cell-spheres
    insanely suboceanic, I dark vestal
    of this evil-eye fire
    and triumphal float

It is uncomfortable, to be stuck
weathercock-like on the pile
of years-entity, empty years of blue:
but if I were to fall from
if I were to become lame I would return then
from departments of hyperuranic traumatologies
well-raised periscope-like
with maxillofacial plastic
ready to integrate into the eternal-ex-visage
hip ready for the uphill slalom

in wide-angle
toward the most recondite spices and delights:
but for some ängströms, one never has access to that pole,
but great goodness and faith for its safety
remains here and there at one's disposal
like meals dispersed throughout the world
within the general prolapse
    in trouble and whines: cycles, periods, eras be given
    to all humans and their kin, if ever
    if still if too much!
Trees move feline there
  where little pearls of up-up-up-up
    entangle in nuptials and whispers with the blue

3

Possible that here "it would seem
    that no story, narrative
machinery, trick, plot, has been
contrived and unrolled with a
    marvelous or tremendous little ending?"
Every forge of firefly-ice
emerged in the dark of the altitudes
where every attempt at orientation is blasphemous
every forge, it is said, is like
    its horrendous relative, the star,
    is a thinking individual, is
        unique furor, never
    passable – dogma, beyond all reproach,
            ultraconjectural love
  Oh saintly unavoided

adjustment to something that does not
evolve if not in the drift
   of its repetitive uniqueness
   gesticulating
   gesticulating in the dark soliciting

Yet what has been
folded onto the milky way dew
   folded to reflect
drop by drop adventures suffering clamors
me chameleonized, bewildered
into votive candles of mutating alphabets,
to imagine myself as spokesman
and cross-bearer for a whole semiculture
on its first legs – maybe – of another nature
sickened woodpecker   even if unworthy
in front of immense excesses of wood

4

Electrified posts unexpected where
   they alarm rail crossings and tracks
on the sure slope, dangerous with dew:
liquiescent crystals of hues
  and minds emerged like periscopes,
  windmill minds, rather pin heads
  rather warbles or assaults of visual presumption,
  coin bank minds of every creatable
  minds emerged by special merit
  at baptisms, in Traian crania –

oh do us the grace of your subtilation
so that we may like *for* one can –
                aspire enquire sane and far
with septum nostrils wide open,
irrepressible asymmetry
causing the most quarrelsome progeny,
allow one's self be invaded by the inaudible
by the extrasounds that only
a new temple expanse appreciates!
Having pulled the sheets up to the neck
the key at hand
    the snag at foot's length,
        a thousand kicks to
        a thousand skull-years
        brilliant with mentality and minds
        in the grass gulf tzompantli-blue
LIFE: "I will be far away, but will not abandon you."

KNICK-KNACKS AND GEL

And there are two in the room's crystal
that at other grades of crystals
breaks, approaches, blends, embeds

And there are two   two old or not even – & friends –
for nothing and of nothing speaking in light accord
they already have poor fatty arteries and bowels
that who knows how difficult find it to machinate
And if they had profiles, they, the friends, would be
in the cut of that infinite crystal in which
november always dares to open wide and afterward imbricate
                avid crystal
                murdering crystal
pressure   presses the essence-colors-of the essence
Two who certainly do not have the wisdom of bonsai,
not zen, but the eye on the yard where
            trotting toward the colors tin cans and penumbra
                Jijo is the name of one   and the other
And in a half-dream they glimpse such a reality
        among tiles and leaves agitated by the crystal
Two united by nothing if not the sense of a certain
    nothingness
but worth as much as the trifles they tell each other
do not even "evoke distant loves"
                even less the memories
            they are memories
            they are nothing
            and warm themselves by the nothing
But it is fatal   it is smashed

in vast and variable crystals   it is november
we intruded a rustling into the crepuscular diptych
      We-they rustle words
      so flowing in their shine so stagnant
         as to become wise
They-we are in any case living even if in honor
of the thin and cold shadows a little at a time
      they adapt – obscure – stupid
Asignificant and maybe mundane is their life
    contracted and swollen the artery the entrails
    they are memories
    they are seated but will trip and fall
    they are these events of windows yards and interiors
    they try to rejoin – and it does not matter –
    an indivisible line crowd – or rather they leave it aside
    they meet again in the valley they adored and were
    distracted
    in the omnipotent unbreatheable levity
    they are distant like two knick-knacks
    and close like rooted figurative conventions
    in the always-more-shadow more-crystal
    They mutter and it is not as if this shines much
      but, ahi closed nose, but there is.

Tiger november meanwhile and always it prowls
throws everything at the feet the astral happy disaster
      uses as arms the moonscythe and sunscythe
it causes the leap of colors the disaccord or chorus –
makes pleural drainage for skins and hyaline strata and gel
pours crystals misplaces a finger of wine
      on the table for two
Two of us are convinced,

in the shadow of a room they accumulate,
two of us on reconnaissance with talk and whispers

Eh eh! Uncle november, this is how you sprinkled us
       with the first cold
       like this you drew us out
    in opportune but inaccessible "there"
    from window to window – we/last ones
    you entwine us in clinking in hillocks in foreignness
– from interior to exterior always more internal
– from interiors with furniture made in paradise
– with transforming butterfly curtains
and I would say knick-knacks and I would say us
it is/so as to know ourselves unseen neither told   nor certified
    and take shelter in gossip in rumeurs
    in spent courtyard jars
while silence grows fierce   the crystal
    and leads in turn to infinity
while the room sides in   the beautiful mind
while two of us side by side move, armed,
    toward pellegrin mosses-colors-mice
    between blows of moonscythe, sunscythe
       Redden, grow verdant, mow
    chew yellowish beyond splashes and serenities,
    turn bluish longish optic modulations
    grows and scouting it steps in line   (with the black)
          puts faith in – ciak – blind.

And I still insist baroquely exhorting
on your grave
       that it is I the world
"Come, rise, I command you"

     No, I have never accepted this waste
      (I mean of hair and nails
      scales secretions breath
      and similar oblations)

     and less still great preservation
     package the wrapping accumulation in marble
     under extreme pressures
      of princes and walk-ons
      of weapons and various masses
      from their own inertia
      and dry heaps

Against fullness – against waste
     and in the grains of savings I hope
     almost invernal nitro in the cavern

(Frozen lakes, beneath mountains)

1

"Lacustrine, marshes almost"
"Yes, yes, it's nothing but a little present"
"It's a pin that fanatically spins"
"Looks like there, in the phases of the Cain star,
but maybe morning from afar"
"For all their modesty, there they assist,
to mediate is their duty, among every disfiguration and
    dissong"
"From the ice they now pull
drippings of blind pupils
placards display booths
flashes of firing squads,
            maimed rectitude toward
            glorifications. But worthless!"

2

"Oh, lecture – bark bark – at least, participate
how heavy it was, how
that focus of waiting
in the most dispersed memory of the pink"

"Here is the crack of language in which I'll do you, give you,
see what light coincidence, not a καιρος
It is enough to place one's self across
become pure inertia, avoid
                    avoiding"

"Perspires, flows, appeals to everything of everyone the oxides
of hardening   of pudor   of lower-the-canvas"
"Yes, that loss in sorcerer's haloes is of lake"
"Have you guessed it, children? Bark bark
          Let's not get too friendly though!"

                    3

(To thrive with the gray)
                    Turning over from the gray
(Suspect, in gray photocolor)

Layers deliciously frozen
or like yesterday like yesterday foggy
of their own exalted essence
     unlimited strength of mind and
     distended reprise in shocks in spots-spies
between fatality and liquiescence
between liquiescences more and more mine
     because slipped from the grip in the gray
slipped from the grip-exhausted branches
I branch light branches almost swarms now
And that which derails into the unfinished down-there.
Call you Stygian, offend you, why?
     Soaking is my foot milking

from the frozen latitude –
soaking sleeping in charge in
        coordination, consubstantiality.

4

Great mistakes you have made
in all the world's things devil!
You should have
kept grain and all in your fist closed-devil
and triumph like a sugar!
But now in the impromptu of the lake
Cain-like in glares like a sugar
in symbols, typical, you perprecipitate into happiness
    Thanks to mundane immaturity
    entities are reinforced, already lost, to lose /
    and launch all their aims
    Great stasis, at last, with lake incarnation
    So dispersed (quiet!) in a veil-tone
                in a freeze-gesture!
    So uniqueness lesions on joyful, you substances of the
    world
    You stop and end-of-the-world
                        stop at the layers, pages

...Like a candid frost evaporated
styge icicle
yet futurable rose of pin in pin
Like a smoke-pure in which..
Or as if amber were to darken to which...
Or paradisiacal stench of saccharids lost in paradise
and all-is-known has to make itself comfortable (unsure)
to accumulate in itself erect
A thousand near-sighted Narcisii revere themselves
are precious in pins and lilacs and cocaine
Everyone a mute dynamic indication
        for reproductions and ruins
Everyone, everything is ready to be constituted,
to hand itself over, in gel
And the infinite love refrigerator findus   gelumel

ΡΟΔΟΝ ΠΟΙΗΣΙΣ ΚΡΥΟΣ

(ANTICYCLONES, WINTERS)

I

See everything that – purple and gold and soft –
       I would almost say regurgitates regurgitates
   does not hold back is happy is mature
   in giving figures tear up figures   other figures
in purple and golds   To sprout golds consider, place hand,
   look outside, take note, to heart, take on,
   be some violence so as to take to heart

   Be another one-on-one with the remote of the purple
      yes, violence in this throat
I listen swimming to all this violence
so primary and uncreated as to be innocent
     but no less murderous - in gold and in purple
There is the murmuring or the touch or the undoing
  purple of no no no   the bell-ringing of the predictor
  Purple is my understanding interreading
   burdens forms mass goes into mass gold and purple
all for you this transparent
mania of destructuralization   but there raise onto the table
the survived

  and the Gewalt blood stain
  raised me like purple filth
twisted me into itself, had lost me in itself, filth.

II

And you await me in the intimate of my gold
and I gaze the intimate of your gold
it is too soft, ambrosiacally poured like ether
    to be gold   it is too distant to be ours
    yet nothing is more nest than this infinite
    perfused in gold, hoed away along the ozone field
          (anticyclones, winters)
substance in which eternity might circulate
    might enjoy become
    one with the scarecrow
    alone but but enabled inhabitant of the hill
    in all golds the azures,
    the encysted abstinences   purple
       the unparalleled incontinence   purple
    the erratic truths the crunchers and the climbers
        Careful of who holds the tomahawk
        to who forges ahead with difficulty
              and – without equal – to disturbances
              fallen from lunar soils
                   from throat to throat.

III

Certainly, I gather in the beauty of the bewilderment,
   with the most granulated supplication
   what there is of silence – so much
   Where surroundings form and acclimatize
   to other subtle rights and duties

Or in dispersed gravel-bank hoarding
   whose glassydark becomes
   what there is of water – so much

   Oriented by insane boldness and deficiencies
   and dark idioms
   precipitated within the idiom
   to multiply its thorns the icicles

It would seem that rarity whistles through the mistletoes of
   the wind and
lash, all those bent withes in the gravel-bank,
   but very mysteriously rebels

Whichever and wherever thing age alleviates
   in front of what will never but never be old,
is not as dried-up as what is generally believed;
   sterile, does not lose vivacity
   fertilizes, in illustrations is stempered

And the moon lights phryne and rime
   in the declining yes
   in passing   unexpected
   with opposition as if taking courage

from where the mountain is more empty
                    gains in fortune
immobile trail on the slope
            [plus goodbye]

Dispersed within a most sweet vocability
                        Eurosia, genius of stones
of hail, dispersed therein Barbara
photoreceptor of the radicularities of lightning

Lucia now emerges from the earthquaked
crystal of the diaphanous
hills   Diva and niña of the Cold
perhaps with a certain following of dour priestlings
    who invite me to lunch, mess hall, warm rations
    She holds a splinter of rays
        that pierce any ubiquity
    in her other hand 9 degrees below zero
        of light gauze-snow,
        feather of bird-already-snow,
    She cannot protect cannot guide
    but will never be of second order
    The scalding that has skinned
    so much of her face and burned away her eyes
    – and why and how are no longer known –
    She was darkness and comes from darkness of her own
    excess
        trimmed with lace of rays
    in the name of the future ΛΟΓΟΣ and all colds to come
    but well aligned, catalogued in snows,
    but eyes everyone and rich tear of attention
    but ruts for numbers and traces
    oh how the dialogue thickens with breaths and piss

hints glimpses!

Lucia: neither mother, nor gifts-in-shadows or in crystal,
    but you are the one who dawns upon what remained
    at your shoulders scarce yearly ravine,
    fainting down down from hill to hill
    fainting up up to the heavens
    Within the ever hungry snare of the cold
    right before you
    we struggle
    and yearn for rations
    and to clear out sweat out remove by hoeing,
    yes, to let everything go, the empty hutches, wide open
    It's gone, no regrets,
    dryness only here and there or shreds,
    flesh-colored in the wild of palates –
    right in the eye the point-blank n
    (desire for numbers, total accounting, of double rations)

(Vien drìote adès la Lùzhia
pi granda e pi scarma de la só istessa imensa bontà)

Admit it, diva Lucia, at your feet – where I know
they lay, me who is blind to all
gradations of light –
that disbands through ravines - where you well know –
humble desire for panegyric.

    Tears well up again. Blow up of
    a single photon. Ω

TABLES, NEWSPAPERS,
PRATALIA DAWN

I

That "the wind feels like snow", that "stagnates, rather"
and "the landlady has a cousin, actually two"
"twins, that resemble her" "and the three of them
confuse everyone"
    "it slams the doors and comes inside very cold"
(december 27 1976
    tavern near the City Gate with the Clock). Inside:
nothing is more vast than those tables
where every historical and metaphysical possibility
emerges, slides out of the sheath and certainly (n.) and
    derivations
        is-and-are among stains
of wine and plate marks   and lustre and fragile discards.
A lustre only slightly presumptive –
from certain tables –
that goes awry and goes off on its own in such a huff
that goes to the distant
following nothing nothing
getting up getting on
a lustre arrived here, to the tables, and anyhow fleeing
    from a well known Emmaus with non-glare lights
    Something changes stupendously in its adherence
    at the lowest point of the table's reality
    low sunshine   "his" shining and broken

It was then confirmed by the two
        pensioners that – here – it is –
        wonderful being closed into the egg of the pensione
        and the tavern
and that: the reflections of the wine-shadow in the glass
        drunk "in such a way that, if the wife comes in,
        it will seem like the first glass," the surroundings
        of such a wine the clues
        of such left-overs of wine –
                leave a little ring imprisoned in the glass –
                everything lets itself
        be caught and dissolved
        including some questions posed, only, because,

And the wind sweeps away death that does not hear us at all
or persuades it to go pick up its pension check
down at the office, if it happens to be open
And the cold sweeps away the horrible millipede
                and '76 with its 366 peduncles of misadventures
And Epiphany will come to sweep away all the holidays
less than the eternal aged of old age homes
        and watchful wives,
        and less than ever twin landladies 1 + 1 + 1 cousins

Fate really oozes from the local
paper, in fact, which does not bring any news
but it is as if it had – oh –
        which living stars, news that makes nothing known,
        news more or less, emanating, abrazed gazette, with
        grazing corner
        that at times even points to a little branch
        that the wind (the one above) has snapped in the woods

and ten threads of grass tread upon by a young boy
to "wounded with sheet-metal"
at a supper for everyone named Mario
to the snows of '76 that maybe
maybe, here in the tavern, the newspaper, worse
of the last five, years or centuries, does it matter? —

Tavern and desire for an empty newspaper
Tavern: you shook off your shoes well, on entering:
      shake off the snows' nudities,
of the gemlike clot under the walking shoes
gather it at the door,
shake your feet
already piled with snow
      if you would like to leave on the right foot

BUT THEN PRATALIA DAWN

Oh logos you let yourself be found
and connected this "this" – let me think
of how great in you is the finding – unique and yours
                   for every thing made unique and its own
– like casting hook and line in the snow
throw and let spin all the whirlwinds up from the snow
and you assign to me a speck of "this"
– Logos, Small like this little Dash and only casually
here in the body of a dash

small like all the forgetting that
seems large – and it is – and it is space
and the space in which you   make dashes and dashes
           make lines
  a whole page of |||||||||||| sleep, a world

|||||||||||||||||| maybe |||| |||| a picket of lines

Is your name Mario like the other hundred in the
   newspaper?
Or is your name, shining from that news, you –
             like that newspaper of which above?
But you desirable bait the nipple
no of course you don't deny it,
extract with hook and line for me from the snow
you snow lamb snow   forgetful for pratalia dawn
you lamb snow

that moving along these lines I stand on, tread on,
and I grow with you small a thousand times like snow
    crystals
and I grow with two lumps of snow under the feet
I wear wooden snow clogs, druck druck,
higher and higher I vacillate
always higher thanks to your small crystal names
                                    I vacillate

Credibility that
does not admit into its splendour, does not allow the return
of even the most present calculation
denied in itself and in the
subthriving blue subsplendours in peace with the shadow
Logos that does not fulminate or cut off or section
Log of undecidables   Log fish-bone
but – like blue – permeates everything of itself, drips
everything, permeates this solstice in very distant snows
otherwise eased, otherwise lived,
permeates our miserable communion rather raises it
toward lost placentae, abandoned to themselves in soft heaps
Log that has no need and that is not there not having need,
but caresses and glorifies stiffening of blue
the nervousity and the microsurprised sopors of the day /

And rich and absolutely inevitable

still does
a pancreas   – so many pancreas here and there of every size
a liver   – just as many (it's necessary) livers in proportion
et cetera   – in the sad pink sack
                et cetera that grind grind sense

mill sense

and they are unreal coral, corals of the deep

of this blue schism

of this appointment in which physical   [fish-bone]

and metaphysical are in violent equilibria   arm wrestling

they search for each other, in snatches, in immobility, in

frantic balances

in the most icethin instabilities

Logos that is not a presence, but that certainly has bases

at the bottom of the coldest creek fingered by ice

but that certainly is Knabe-pebble $^{\log}$ of the ice $^{\log}$ snow

or it is Knabe of the bush it is resource of the Gestell

or of the plastic bag

of the balloon in which blow imps

it is Knabe whose curls of moss-ice spill over ably

they evaporate gold in the mouth of everything

but arrive also as warm and dear pisses also arrive

from the crib that was the crib of emptiness

Logos unintimidating and unsmiling

but winning in all the single phosphoric DNA

of these many, active solitudes

Mathesis of the mandible in lethargy, of the tear

gummy in the pink, of the nitro, of the blue salts

$^{\log}$DEUS $^{\log}$EGO $^{\log}$ICE $^{\log}$SKIES

that, very pure specters, thicken, invade

Ranks and hives, losing, of all mathematics,

navel, matronid, sinusoid

jokes and summersaults of little number-letters   in ice

in blue

By now a sense – the blue says (Knabe) is foreseen

in the sense that isn't there   in the Logos that isn't there

Hurry in drinking even to the most driest-freeze

76

jug, Samaritan, ventana,
to the most apprenticed and snowed (there, skiing) of the
blue

He dies of memory and stupor

and in memory and stupor retires and resutures
A sip then, before light

of twig and branch,
of the star that has lost its way for this and that,
of the star worthy of us in the evening...

Mathesis link that advances abundance
of Wolves-were and snows-Knabe
Knabe nude, nude in words, wounded by mini-
hooks algebraic burrs numerical fish-bones
for the immensity of circling understandings
for the zero of understandings are dispersed
sly wants, joys of bicycles, straw irradiations,
turdcaterpillars in fallen
strata of valleys and rest
beneath great satellites of rest –
Or everything is afterall fractured in discontinuous
surveillance, cut with an axe...

Sad Relaxed Abandoned Coerced
maybe there to react or definitively quit
the universal heap overflows beyond any obstacle...
But then it is almost thaumaturgical work
even this spine of a spectre, of résumé
left behind behind
here in the consumptive, left by all the freezes the rivers
the silecaeus furrows trace-bearers,

from the Simple Reverb from the Tenerello
       that is endearing and stubborn
       in choosing and displaying
       in flower stems pollen of memories
       to interweave Mneme with Mneme
       to extend the slaughterhouse
the blood flow in warm coral and sweet stench

Mneme slaughterhouse   so disgustingly mismatched
stuck among themselves   respectively never been

And He hit bulls eye, at one time, when he cashed-out
the game of bocce
with the cue ball
           and flashed the pineal gland!

SIMPLE FUTURES — OR ANTERIOR?

Logos, in every crystal of glorious snow brine
even if maybe you are nothing more than an hypothesis
━━◁　　　　than a Witz an impulse of subtle anger
Unverifiable connection between frosts and frosts
　　points of sight and points of light

Not to repent　　　　not say too much　　　　not gather up
　　too much　　　　　　　　　　be stalk and branch
　　　　sparked by immobility into drops
　　　　to invent　　to hollow out　　to entrap

The dawning and varied nudity of being
　　I will soon mimic, and the meanest touch, the vigorous
　　note,
　　negated in the cold
　　contamination and clarity ciliated slightly in this direction

Logos　– not important mutisms nor rumours
　　– not　　false notes nor dwarf-colours crowded stumbles
　　– not　　your other possible importance
　　　　　　　　　　　　nor your death
　　　　　　　　　　　　nor your loss
　　that I took on in profusion
Perfusion of cold and little dazzling fevers
　　　　　　　　　　and infinite immicrobation
perfusion vein to vein – from poverty to poverty
　　Every step　　displaces and grasps like the turn of a screw
　　every voice　　suffocates sweetly useless

79

every gaze   pokes its eyes out

but so as to gain the most for you and the
most terrible starrity, like
          of snow on the edge of the   of the indicated
                                               movement
                                               But humiliated.

NOTES

These poems were composed mostly at the same time as those in *Il Galateo in Bosco*, between 1975 and 1978. Others were added in subsequent years, until 1981. The present collection could then be said to represent the second part of a highly improbable trilogy that was announced with *Galateo*. It stands here as a contrast or residue, a north that through various types of hilly movements dissipates into dolomitic space and its geometries. As such, it moves toward snows and abstractions, through fogs, cold, gelatings, and little if any narrative.

Under the name of logos stands every insistent and benign force of understanding, communication and interconnection that cross reality fantasy words, and also tends to "gift" them, put them into direct relationship with a starting point (?). And who knows what else. The Greek – or pseudo-Greek – locutions at the end or near the end of many poems, are meant to work as "converted" or reflected titles, reflections.

FOSFENI
Vortexes of signs and luminous points that are seen by closing one's eyes (and squeezing) as well as in pathological cases. From "La Pasqua a Pieve di Soligo" in *Pasque* (Milano: Mondadori, 1973) p. 57.

LIKE LAST SUPPERS
"Miniorgasm in atchoo": makes reference to the comparison made by some psychoanalysts between a sneeze and sexual orgasm. "Gel": here, as in the rest of the book, it has the value of "frigid gelatin." ΘΕΩΡΙΑ ΚΡΥΟΣ: theory, but also procession, and gelo-crystalized-gel.

SILICA, CARBON, SCAFFOLDERS
Carbon and silica understood as sound symbols; minerality that supports life and pure minerality, but awaiting developments from S.F. (especially as it relates to the "logos in silica" of calculators). – "Interranges": polydirectional unions, almost like a connective network, temporary and uncertain. Neurons with their ramifications and synapse. – "Number one number two": as in a still remembered goliardic and popular song.

(LOGHION)
usually understood as "unforgettable proverb" but here to be taken also with a slight sense of lesser or complete non-existence. – "bubola": local dialect for firefly, "borboletta": Portuguese for butterfly.

MARTENS, PAINS, ΛΟΓΙΛ
poem written almost as extracted from the book *Pasque*. – "Sghirlo": local dialect for a small vortex. – "Fureghina": local dialect, referring to something that finds its way into every situation in a gracious but astute manner.

THE TEACHER MORCHET LIVES
the teacher is the protagonist of the long poem "The Mysteries of Pedagogy" (in *Pasque*). There too there is a mention of the Reading Center which today no longer exists.

EUROSIA
according to local belief, is a saint who protects from hail. – "the vigil": refers to the therapeutic vigils under the influence of hallucinogens, similar to those that take place in Mexico. See the experiences of Maria Sabina. – "from roots ... if one wants it": extracted from roots, etc.

DISTRUST THROAT, BODY, MOVEMENTS, THEATRE

"Ch. M., J.M.L. and others": poets who make use of the phon-ico-semantic aspect of poetry in their "compositions", under-stood primarily as performance. – "Dynamic directions": to be equated with "agogic directions" plus "dynamic signs", in the sense that such expressions have in music. See further along also in "(Frozen lakes, beneath mountains)".

(AT GHÈNE)

In remote times, "Ghène" the host's nickname.

WELL DISPOSED SILENCES

"οὐδεν": it is no longer worth much by mistake, even if it recalls the theme of giving without expecting anything in return.

PERISCOPES

"Liquid crystals": think about their qualities – now-a-days much exploited even as objects for everyday use. – "Traian cra-nia": ref. Traian's privilege , canto XX of Dante's Paradise. – "Tzompantli": place where in Aztec Mexico skulls from human sacrifices were stored.

VOCABILITY, PHOTONS

December 13th, Lucia gives start to the cold. – "Lùzhia": she "vien drìote", follows like a shadow. It refers to an old woman, very tall and thin ("scarma"), very generous, but dead and for-gotten for decades.

TABLES, NEWSPAPERS, PRATALIA DAWN

These are the snowy tillable plains that symbolize the white page, according to the old riddle from Verona. – "City Gate with the clock": in Serravalle, Vittorio Veneto, but in many other towns as well.

LINES IN THE SPECTRE (LUMINOUS)

"Logos," smaller and smaller, is miniaturized as far as a cantankerous indication of the logarithm. With this value it then influences names, places, sensations, it pierces them or hooks on to them. – "Knabe" is most of all the "golden boy" of the Christmas song, and as such he too is logos. – "Gestell": in the heideggerian sense, maybe. In any case, frame. – "Samaritan": she stands by the frozen well with the broken jug. "Ventana": window. – "Pineal gland": the place of encounter par excellence (of Cartesian memory). It is not a "steady point", it is a flashing and intermittent light. – Some of the figures are an improper rendering or a distant allusive trace of some wonderful topological features.

Andrea Zanzotto (1921) is regarded as the major living Italian poet. He is the author of many volumes of poetry among which are *Dietro il paesaggio* (1951), *IX Ecloghe* (1962), *La Beltà* (1968), *Pasque* (1973), *Fosfeni* (1983), and *Idioma* (1986), *Meteo* (1996) and *Sovrimpressioni* (2001). He has received several major literary prizes, including the Viareggio (1979), the Librex-Montale (1983), and the Feltrinelli (1987). This translation of *Fosfeni* is the first of a full-length volume to appear in English.

Pasquale Verdicchio teaches at the University of California, San Diego. He has translated the work of Pier Paolo Pasolini, Giorgio Caproni, Antonio Porta, Alda Merini, Valerio Magrelli, and other Italian poets. His own most recent book of poetry is *This Nothing's Place* (Guernica, 2008).